CHRISTINE HAGGINS

Paul Apostle Biography

From Persecutor to Preacher, The Remarkable Life and Ministry of Paul, the Apostle

Contents

INTRODUCTION

One of the most significant individuals in the history of Christianity is the apostle Paul. His life and ministry had a profound impact on the early church, and his writings have continued to shape Christian theology and practice for centuries. Yet, Paul's journey to become a follower of Christ was not a smooth one. He began as a zealous persecutor of the early Christians, but through a dramatic encounter with Jesus, he was transformed into a passionate preacher of the gospel.

In this book, "Paul Apostle Biography: From Persecutor to Preacher," we will explore the remarkable life and ministry of Paul, from his upbringing as a Pharisee to his missionary journeys and eventual martyrdom. We will examine his theological teachings, such as justification by faith and the role of grace, and the impact they had on the early church and continue to have on Christian thought today.

Throughout this book, we will delve into the historical and cultural context in which Paul lived, and how his experiences shaped his perspectives and teachings. We will also explore the challenges he faced, including imprisonment and persecution, and how he remained steadfast in his faith despite these obstacles.

Whether you are a scholar of early Christianity, a student

of theology, or simply curious about the life of this influential figure, this book offers a comprehensive look at the extraordinary journey of Paul from persecutor to preacher. Through this exploration, we hope to gain a deeper understanding of the man, his ministry, and his enduring legacy.

Purpose of the Book

The purpose of this book is to provide a comprehensive and accessible account of the life and ministry of the apostle Paul, with a particular focus on his transformation from a persecutor of early Christians to a passionate preacher of the gospel.

By examining the historical and cultural context in which Paul lived and wrote, this book aims to shed light on the factors that shaped his perspectives and teachings. It also aims to explore the enduring impact of Paul's teachings on Christian theology and practice.

Through this book, we hope to provide readers with a deeper understanding of the man behind the letters and to show how his experiences and insights can still be relevant to our lives today. We believe that Paul's journey from persecutor to preacher offers valuable insights into the power of redemption and transformation, and can serve as an inspiration for all those who seek to live a life of faith and service.

Ultimately, our goal is to provide a rich and engaging narrative that will appeal to both scholars and general readers alike and contribute to the ongoing conversation about the life and legacy of this remarkable figure. Whether you are a seasoned theologian or simply curious about the life of this influential figure, we hope that this book will offer new insights and perspectives on the life and ministry of the apostle Paul.

Background

Before diving into Paul's transformation from persecutor to preacher, it is important to have a general understanding of his life and ministry.

Paul, also known as Saul, was born in Tarsus in Cilicia (modern-day Turkey) around the year AD 5. He was a Jew and a Roman citizen, and he grew up in a devout Pharisee family. As a young man, he was sent to Jerusalem to study under Gamaliel, one of the most respected Jewish teachers of the time.

Despite his religious education, Paul initially viewed the early Christian movement with suspicion and hostility. He even played a role in the persecution and execution of early Christians. However, his life was transformed after he had a dramatic encounter with Jesus on the road to Damascus. This experience led him to become a fervent believer in Jesus Christ and a passionate preacher of the gospel.

Paul's missionary journeys were crucial in spreading Christianity throughout the Roman Empire. He traveled extensively throughout the eastern Mediterranean, establishing churches and preaching the gospel to both Jews and Gentiles. He faced significant opposition and persecution during his travels, but he remained steadfast in his faith and continued to spread the message of salvation through Christ.

Paul's teachings on topics such as justification by faith, the role of grace, and the Holy Spirit have had a profound impact on Christian theology and practice. His letters, which make up a significant portion of the New Testament, have been studied and debated for centuries, and they continue to inspire and challenge Christians around the world.

Overall, Paul's life and ministry represent a remarkable

journey of transformation and redemption, and his legacy continues to influence Christian thought and practice to this day.

Chapter 1: Pharisee's Upbringing

This section provides an in-depth look at the upbringing of the man who would become one of the most influential figures in the history of Christianity. Born into a Jewish family in Tarsus, a city in the Roman province of Cilicia, Paul grew up in a devout Pharisee household.

The Pharisees were a Jewish sect known for their strict adherence to religious law and their emphasis on personal piety. Paul's parents were likely deeply committed to their faith, and they would have instilled in him a strong sense of Jewish identity and a reverence for the Torah.

Despite his upbringing, Paul's early years were marked by a certain degree of cultural and religious diversity. Tarsus was a cosmopolitan city with a significant Greek and Roman population, and Paul would have been exposed to a range of different ideas and beliefs. This exposure to different cultures and worldviews may have contributed to his later ability to bridge the gap between Jews and Gentiles in his ministry.

As a young man, Paul was sent to Jerusalem to study under Gamaliel, a prominent Jewish teacher and, member of the Sanhedrin. This education would have been rigorous and demanding, and it would have prepared Paul for a life of leadership within the Jewish community.

Early Life and Education

Paul's early life and education were shaped by several events that would have a profound impact on his later ministry. Born into a Jewish family in Tarsus, a major city in the Roman province of Cilicia, Paul would have grown up in a culturally diverse environment, with exposure to both Jewish and Greco-Roman traditions.

As a young boy, Paul would have learned the Torah and other Jewish scriptures from his parents, who were likely devout Pharisees. He would have also received a general education, including reading, writing, and arithmetic, which was available to both boys and girls in Tarsus.

At around the age of 13, Paul would have been sent to Jerusalem to study under a prominent Jewish teacher. In Paul's case, this teacher was Gamaliel, a respected member of the Sanhedrin and a leading figure in Jewish scholarship. Under Gamaliel's tutelage, Paul would have received a rigorous education in Jewish law and tradition, as well as exposure to Greek philosophy and rhetoric.

Paul's education in Jerusalem would have been both challenging and prestigious. He would have been part of a small, elite group of students who were being groomed for leadership roles within the Jewish community. This education would have equipped Paul with a deep knowledge of Jewish law and tradition, as well as critical thinking skills and the ability to communicate persuasively.

Paul's early life and education played a significant role in shaping his later ministry. His upbringing in a diverse cultural environment, his Jewish education, and his exposure to Greek philosophy and rhetoric all contributed to the unique perspective he brought to his ministry. By understanding these formative years, we can gain a deeper appreciation for the factors that shaped Paul's perspectives and teachings, and for the incredible journey of transformation that he would undergo later in life.

The Influence of Judaism

Judaism played a significant role in shaping Paul's worldview and his approach to ministry. As a Pharisee, Paul would have been deeply steeped in Jewish tradition and law, and he would have had a strong sense of Jewish identity and pride.

One of the key aspects of Judaism that would have influenced Paul's ministry was the concept of covenant. The idea of a covenant between God and his chosen people was central to Jewish theology, and it provided the foundation for the Jewish understanding of salvation and redemption. Paul's understanding of the covenant would be an important element of his later teachings about salvation through faith in Jesus Christ.

Another important aspect of Judaism that would have influenced Paul's ministry was the emphasis on holiness and righteousness. Jewish law and tradition placed a strong emphasis on personal piety and moral purity, and Paul's early Pharisaic training would have reinforced these values. This emphasis on holiness would later inform Paul's teachings about the importance of living a righteous life and avoiding sin.

Despite his deep roots in Judaism, Paul's encounter with Jesus on the road to Damascus would lead him to a radical transformation in his understanding of God and his relationship with humanity. Nevertheless, his Jewish background remained an important element of his ministry, and it would continue to shape his teachings and his approach to ministry throughout his life.

The influence of Judaism on Paul's ministry highlights the complex interplay between tradition and transformation in the development of Christian theology. By understanding how Paul's Jewish background informed his teachings, we can gain a deeper appreciation for the rich and diverse theological traditions that have shaped the history of Christianity.

Becoming a Pharisee

Paul's journey toward becoming a Pharisee began with his upbringing in a devout Jewish family. As a young boy, Paul would have been raised with a strong sense of Jewish identity and a deep respect for Jewish tradition and law.

However, it was during his studies in Jerusalem under the prominent Jewish teacher Gamaliel that Paul fully embraced the Pharisaic tradition. The Pharisees were a sect within Judaism that emphasized strict adherence to Jewish law and tradition, and they saw themselves as the protectors of Jewish identity in the face of Hellenistic and Roman influence.

Under Gamaliel's tutelage, Paul would have been exposed to the rich intellectual and spiritual traditions of the Pharisees, including their sophisticated understanding of Jewish law and their commitment to personal piety and moral purity. He would have learned the intricacies of the Torah and the Talmud, as well as the various commentaries and interpretations that had developed over centuries of Jewish scholarship.

As Paul matured in his understanding of the Pharisaic tradition, he became increasingly committed to its ideals and principles. He embraced the Pharisees' strict code of conduct, which included practices such as fasting, ritual purity, and tithing. He also came to believe that the Pharisees held the key to preserving Jewish identity in a world that was increasingly hostile to Jewish tradition and values.

Paul's journey toward becoming a Pharisee highlights the deep commitment that he had to Jewish tradition and identity. It also underscores the complex interplay between tradition and transformation in the development of Christian theology, as Paul's later encounter with Jesus would lead him to a radical transformation in his understanding of God and his relationship with vanity.

Chapter 2: Saul the Persecutor

This section explores the early years of Saul, before he became the renowned Apostle Paul. This chapter delves into the period when Saul was known as a zealous persecutor of Christians, and provides insight into the factors that contributed to his transformation into one of the most significant individuals in the history of Christianity.

Saul's role as a persecutor of Christians is a critical part of his story, as it highlights the stark contrast between his earlier life and his later ministry. At this stage of his life, Saul was deeply committed to the Pharisaic tradition and saw Christianity as a threat to Jewish identity and tradition. He actively sought out and persecuted early Christian communities, going so far as to oversee the stoning of Stephen, one of the first Christian martyrs.

Despite his violent opposition to Christianity, Saul's encounter with Jesus on the road to Damascus would lead him to a dramatic conversion and a radical transformation in his understanding of God and his relationship to humanity. This transformation would ultimately lead Saul to become one of the most influential figures in the development of Christian theology and thought.

The story of Saul's persecution of Christians highlights the complex and often fraught relationships between different religious traditions, as well as the beliefs and practices can shape individual identities and actions. By exploring Saul's early years as a persecutor, we gain a deeper appreciation for the profound transformation that he underwent, and the enduring impact that his life and ministry would have on the development of Christianity.

Persecuting Early Christians

Saul's persecution of early Christians was a defining moment in his early life and career. As a zealous Pharisee, he saw the Christian movement as a threat to Jewish identity and tradition, and he was determined to stamp it out.

Saul's persecution of Christians was characterized by violence and intimidation. He oversaw the stoning of Stephen, one of the first Christian martyrs, and he actively sought out and arrested other followers of Jesus. He was relentless in his efforts to suppress the Christian movement, and he became known as a feared and hated figure among the early Christian communities.

Despite the violent nature of his persecution, Saul believed that he was acting in accordance with Jewish law and tradition. He saw the Christian movement as a dangerous heresy that threatened the very foundations of Judaism, and he believed that it was his duty to protect Jewish identity and tradition from this perceived threat.

Saul's persecution of early Christians highlights the deep divisions and tensions that existed within Jewish society at the time. It also underscores the complex interplay between religious belief and political power, as Saul's commitment to the

Pharisaic tradition led him to use his authority and influence to suppress a religious movement that he saw as a threat to Jewish identity and tradition.

Saul's persecution of early Christians would play a critical role in his transformation into the Apostle Paul. His encounter with Jesus on the road to Damascus would challenge his beliefs and assumptions, and would ultimately lead him to a radical transformation in his understanding of God and his relationship with humanity.

The Conversion Experience

The conversion experience of Saul, later known as Paul, was a pivotal moment in his life and ministry. According to the biblical account, Saul was on his way to Damascus to continue his persecution of Christians when he had a powerful encounter with the risen Christ.

During this encounter, Saul was struck blind and heard the voice of Jesus asking him why he was persecuting him. This experience left Saul shaken and confused, and he was led by his companions to Damascus, where he remained blind and fasting for three days.

After three days, a man named Ananias was sent by God to lay his hands on Saul and pray for his healing. At that moment, Saul's sight was restored, and he was filled with the Holy Spirit. This experience would lead to a radical transformation in Saul's understanding of God and his relationship to humanity, and would ultimately shape the trajectory of his life and ministry.

The conversion experience of Saul is a powerful example of the transformative power of faith. It highlights the ways in which our beliefs and assumptions can be challenged and transformed by encounters with the divine, and it underscores the importance of being open to new experiences and perspectives.

Saul's conversion experience also highlights the ways in which our past experiences and actions can shape our future. Despite his early role as a persecutor of Christians, Saul was able to embrace a new understanding of God's grace and forgiveness, and to become one of the most influential figures in the development of Christian theology and thought.

Saul's conversion experience serves as a model for all Christians, reminding us of the importance of being open to the transformative power of faith, and of the ways in which our past experiences and actions can be redeemed and transformed by God's grace.

Ananias and the Road to Damascus

The story of Ananias and the Road to Damascus is a critical part of Saul's conversion experience. After his encounter with Jesus, Saul was left blinded and in need of assistance. It was Ananias who was sent by God to heal him and guide him on his journey of faith.

Ananias was a devout disciple of Jesus living in Damascus. When he received a vision from God instructing him to go to Saul and lay his hands on him, he was understandably hesitant. After all, Saul was known as a fierce persecutor of Christians, and many in the community feared him.

Despite his reservations, however, Ananias obeyed God's command and went to Saul. He laid his hands on him, prayed for his healing, and proclaimed the gospel to him. In that moment, Saul's sight was restored, and he was filled with the Holy Spirit.

The encounter between Ananias and Saul is a powerful example of the transformative power of faith and obedience. Ananias was willing to step out in faith and follow God's call, even when it was difficult and scary. His obedience played a critical role in Saul's conversion experience, and ultimately helped to shape the trajectory of Christian history.

The story of Ananias and the Road to Damascus also highlights the importance of community and support in the journey of faith. Ananias was a trusted and respected member of the Christian community, and his presence and guidance were critical in Saul's journey of faith. In the same way, we all need the support and guidance of others as we navigate the challenges and complexities of the Christian life.

Overall, the story of Ananias and the Road to Damascus serves as a powerful reminder of the transformative power of faith and obedience, and of the importance of community and support in the journey of faith.

Chapter 3: Paul's Early Ministry

After his conversion experience on the road to Damascus, Saul began a new chapter in his life as a follower of Jesus Christ. Initially, he spent some time in Damascus, preaching the gospel and confounding his former colleagues in the Jewish community with his newfound zeal for Christ.

Eventually, Saul traveled to Jerusalem, where he met with the disciples and began his early ministry. Despite some initial hesitations and doubts from the disciples, Saul quickly became a powerful advocate for the gospel, preaching and teaching with authority and conviction.

This chapter will explore the early years of Paul's ministry, as he established himself as a leader in the early Christian church and began to shape the trajectory of Christian theology and thought. We will examine his interactions with the disciples, his early preaching and teaching, and the challenges he faced as he sought to spread the gospel to the world.

Through our exploration of Paul's early ministry, we will gain a deeper understanding of the foundations of the Christian faith, and the ways in which the early church grappled with the complexities and challenges of spreading the gospel in a world that was often hostile and resistant to their message. We will also gain insight into the character and vision of apostle Paul, and the ways in which his ministry and teachings continue to shape our understanding of God and the world around us.

The Beginnings of Paul's Preaching

After his conversion experience and his time in Damascus, Paul began preaching the gospel in earnest. He was initially met with skepticism and suspicion from both the disciples and the broader Jewish community, many of whom remembered him as a fierce persecutor of Christians.

Despite these challenges, Paul remained steadfast in his commitment to Christ and his mission to spread the gospel. He began preaching in synagogues throughout the region, arguing persuasively from the scriptures that Jesus was indeed the Messiah.

One of the most notable early examples of Paul's preaching can be found in Acts 9:20-22, which describes his preaching in the synagogues of Damascus:

"At once he began to preach in the synagogues that Jesus is the Son of God. All those who heard him were astonished and asked, 'Isn't he the man who raised havoc in Jerusalem among those who call on this name? And hasn't he come here to take them as prisoners to the chief priests?' Yet Saul grew more and more powerful and baffled the Jews living in Damascus by proving that Jesus is the Messiah."

Through his preaching, Paul quickly established himself as a powerful advocate for the gospel, and his message began to spread throughout the region. He continued to preach and teach, both in synagogues and in other settings, and his influence and impact continued to grow.

The Missionary Journeys

The missionary journeys of Paul were a critical part of his ministry and played a significant role in the spread of Christianity throughout the Mediterranean world. After spending some time in Antioch, where he was commissioned by the church to undertake a mission to the Gentiles, Paul set out on his first missionary journey.

This journey, which is described in detail in Acts 13-14, took Paul and his companions to Cyprus, Pisidian Antioch, Iconium, Lystra, and Derbe. Along the way, Paul preached the gospel, established churches, and worked to strengthen the faith of believers. He also encountered significant opposition, including from those who were jealous of his success and those who were committed to opposing the spread of Christianity.

Despite these challenges, Paul remained steadfast in his mission, and his preaching and teaching continued to gain traction. After returning to Antioch, he set out on a second missionary journey, which took him to cities including Philippi, Thessalonica, Berea, Athens, and Corinth.

This journey was marked by both successes and setbacks. In Philippi, Paul and Silas were imprisoned after casting out a demon from a slave girl, but were ultimately released after an earthquake shook the prison and opened the doors. In Athens, Paul faced significant resistance from the philosophers who were suspicious of his teachings.

Paul continued to preach and teach, and his message continued to resonate with many. He established churches throughout the region, including in Corinth, where he spent 18 months teaching and strengthening the faith of believers.

Paul's third missionary journey took him back to many

of the same cities he had visited on his previous journeys. He continued to establish churches, preach the gospel, and work to strengthen the faith of believers. Along the way, he also encountered significant opposition and faced challenges, including a riot in Ephesus.

Paul's missionary journeys were marked by remarkable success, and his teachings and influence continue to shape Christian theology and thought to this day. Through his commitment to spreading the gospel and his willingness to endure hardships and persecution, Paul demonstrated the transformative power of faith and the enduring impact of a life dedicated to serving God.

The Council of Jerusalem

The Council of Jerusalem was a significant event in the early Christian Church, and it played a crucial role in the spread of Christianity to Gentile believers. The council was called to address a dispute that had arisen in the church about whether Gentile converts needed to be circumcised and follow Jewish customs in order to be saved.

At the council, which is described in detail in Acts 15, Paul and Barnabas presented their case for allowing Gentile believers to be accepted into the church without having to follow Jewish customs. James, the brother of Jesus and the leader of the Jerusalem church, also spoke in favor of this position.

After much debate and discussion, the council ultimately agreed that Gentile believers did not need to be circumcised or follow Jewish customs in order to be saved. Instead, they were to be encouraged to abstain from certain practices, such as eating meat sacrificed to idols and consuming blood, that were considered offensive to Jewish believers.

The decision of the council was a significant moment in the history of the church, as it marked a shift away from the idea that salvation was only available to those who followed Jewish customs. It also helped to pave the way for the spread of Christianity to Gentile believers throughout the Roman Empire.

For Paul, the decision of the council was a validation of his teachings and his mission to preach the gospel to the Gentiles. It also helped to establish him as a key figure in the early Christian Church, and his influence continued to grow in the years that followed.

Chapter 4: Paul's Theology

This Chapter focuses on Paul's theology, which is a crucial aspect of his teachings and ministry. Paul's theology is centered around the person and work of Jesus Christ, and it is grounded in his understanding of the Old Testament Scriptures and his experiences as an apostle.

Paul's theology can be understood in several key areas, including his understanding of salvation, the role of the law, the nature of the church, and eschatology. These themes are woven throughout his letters to the early Christian communities, and they continue to be significant for Christian theology today.

In this chapter, we will explore the key elements of Paul's theology and how they relate to the broader context of the early Christian Church. We will examine how Paul's theology developed over time, and how it was shaped by his experiences as an apostle and his interactions with other early Christian leaders.

Our goal in this chapter is to gain a deeper understanding of the theological foundations of Paul's teachings, and how they continue to shape Christian thought and practice today. By exploring the nuances of Paul's theology, we can gain a richer appreciation for his contributions to the Christian tradition and the enduring relevance of his teachings for contemporary believers.

Justification by Faith

One of the most significant themes in Paul's theology is justification by faith, which refers to the idea that salvation is a gift of God that is received by faith in Jesus Christ, rather than through obedience to the law or good works.

Paul's emphasis on justification by faith is rooted in his own experience of conversion, in which he came to understand that salvation is not earned through obedience to the law, but is a free gift of God's grace. In his letters, he argues that all people are sinful and fall short of God's standards, and that no one can be justified by their own efforts.

Instead, Paul argues that righteousness is imputed to believers through faith in Jesus Christ. This means that when a person puts their trust in Jesus, they are counted as righteous in God's sight, not because of their own merits, but because of Christ's sacrificial death and resurrection.

Paul's emphasis on justification by faith was controversial in his own time, as it challenged the Jewish belief that righteousness could be earned through obedience to the law. However, it has become a central tenet of Christian theology, and it continues to be a source of inspiration and comfort to believers around the world.

For Paul, justification by faith is not simply a matter of intellectual belief, but also involves a transformation of the heart and a commitment to a new way of life. He emphasizes the importance of faith, love, and obedience in the life of the believer, and his teachings continue to challenge and inspire Christians to this day.

The Role of Grace

Another key element of Paul's theology is his emphasis on grace, which refers to the unmerited favor of God towards humanity. Paul teaches that salvation is a gift of God's grace, and it cannot be earned through human effort or good works.

Paul's understanding of grace is rooted in his own experience of conversion, in which he came to understand that he was saved not because of his own righteousness, but because of God's grace. This understanding of grace is reflected in his letters to the early Christian communities, where he emphasizes the importance of faith in Jesus Christ as the means of receiving God's grace.

Paul's teaching on grace also includes the idea of forgiveness, which is made possible through Christ's sacrifice on the cross. He emphasizes that all people are sinners in need of forgiveness, and that the only way to receive this forgiveness is through faith in Jesus.

Paul's emphasis on grace is significant because it challenges the idea that salvation can be earned through good works or human effort. Instead, it emphasizes the central role of God's grace in the process of salvation, and highlights the importance of faith and trust in God's provision.

The concept of grace continues to be a central theme in Christian theology, and it remains a source of inspiration and comfort to believers around the world. Paul's teaching on grace highlights the transformative power of God's love, and the hope that is available to all who put their trust in Him.

The Holy Spirit and Christian Living

The Holy Spirit is another central element of Paul's theology, and he teaches that the Spirit plays a key role in the life of the believer. Paul teaches that when a person puts their faith in Jesus Christ, they receive the gift of the Holy Spirit, who guides them in their Christian walk and empowers them to live a pleasing life to God.

According to Paul, the Holy Spirit is the source of spiritual gifts and enables believers to live in accordance with God's will. He emphasizes the importance of the Holy Spirit in transforming the lives of believers, and in equipping them for ministry and service in the church.

Paul also teaches that the Holy Spirit is a source of unity within the church, and that believers should strive to maintain the unity of the Spirit through love, humility, and a willingness to serve one another.

The role of the Holy Spirit in Christian living is significant because it emphasizes the importance of a personal relationship with God, and highlights the transformative power of the Spirit in the life of the believer. It also underscores the importance of community within the church, and the need for believers to support and encourage one another as they seek to follow Christ.

Paul's teaching on the Holy Spirit continues to be a source of inspiration and guidance for Christians around the world, and it serves as a reminder of the central role of the Spirit in the believer's life.

Chapter 5: Paul's Later Years

As we turn our attention to the later years of Paul's life, we see a man who has experienced great hardship and persecution in his efforts to spread the gospel message. Despite these challenges, Paul remains committed to his calling and continues to minister to the early Christian communities, providing them with guidance and encouragement as they seek to follow Christ.

During this period, Paul's ministry takes on a more pastoral focus, as he works to establish and strengthen the churches that he has founded. He writes letters to the churches, offering them guidance and instruction on matters such as Christian living, spiritual gifts, and the importance of unity within the church.

We also see Paul continuing to face opposition and criticism from those who are opposed to his message, and he experiences further hardships such as imprisonment and physical suffering. Despite these challenges, however, Paul remains steadfast in his faith and continues to serve as an example of Christian perseverance and commitment.

In this chapter, we will explore the later years of Paul's life, including his continued ministry to the early Christian communities, his writings to the churches, and his experiences of persecution and hardship. We will see how Paul's faith and dedication to the gospel message continue to inspire and challenge believers today, and how his legacy as one of the greatest missionaries and theologians in Christian history continues to impact the world today.

Imprisonment and Trials

In the later years of his ministry, Paul experiences a number of trials and imprisonments, which serve as a testament to his unwavering commitment to his faith and to his mission to spread the gospel message. Despite the challenges he faces, Paul remains resolute and continues to minister to the early Christian communities, even while imprisoned.

One of the most well-known imprisonments that Paul faces is his imprisonment in Rome, which is documented in the New Testament book of Acts. While in prison, Paul continues to write letters to the churches, offering them guidance and encouragement even while he himself is facing significant hardship.

Throughout his imprisonment and trials, Paul remains steadfast in his faith and continues to trust in God's plan for his life. He encourages the early Christians to persevere in their own faith, and he provides them with guidance on how to live a pleasing life to God.

For believers today, Paul's example of faith in the face of hardship and persecution serves as an inspiration and a challenge to remain committed to our own faith, even in the midst of difficult circumstances. His letters from prison continue to be a source of encouragement and instruction for Christians around the world, and his legacy as a faithful servant of God remains an inspiration to us all.

The Prison Epistles

The Prison Epistles refer to the letters that Paul wrote while he was imprisoned, likely in Rome. These letters, which include Ephesians, Philippians, Colossians, and Philemon, offer insight into Paul's theology and his pastoral concern for the early Christian communities.

In these letters, Paul emphasizes the importance of unity within the church and encourages believers to work together for the sake of the gospel message. He also emphasizes the importance of living a pleasing life to God, and offers guidance on how to live a life marked by love, compassion, and humility.

Perhaps most importantly, the Prison Epistles provide insight into Paul's understanding of Christ and his role in the salvation of humanity. In these letters, Paul emphasizes the centrality of Christ and his sacrificial death on the cross, which he sees as the ultimate act of love and redemption.

The Prison Epistles offer a rich and nuanced view of Paul's theology and his pastoral concern for the early Christian communities. They continue to be a source of inspiration and guidance for believers today, and their impact on Christian theology and spirituality cannot be overstated.

Martyrdom and Legacy

Paul's ministry ended with his martyrdom, likely in Rome, sometime around AD 64-67. He was executed by the Roman authorities for his outspoken and controversial teachings about Christ, which were seen as a threat to the stability of the Roman Empire.

Despite his untimely death, Paul's legacy has endured for

thousands of years. His teachings and writings continue to inspire and challenge believers around the world, and his life serves as a powerful example of faith in the face of adversity and persecution.

In many ways, Paul's martyrdom served to solidify his reputation as a faithful servant of God, and his death has been interpreted by many as a powerful testimony to the truth of his teachings. His letters, which offer guidance on everything from Christian living to theological doctrine, continue to be read and studied by scholars and laypeople alike, and his impact on Christian theology and spirituality cannot be overstated.

Paul's legacy also extends beyond his writings and teachings. Throughout his ministry, he was instrumental in establishing early Christian communities throughout the Mediterranean world, and many of these communities continue to exist today. His work in spreading the gospel message paved the way for the growth and development of the early Christian church, and his influence can still be felt in the modern church.

Paul's life and legacy are a testament to the power of faith and the enduring impact of one individual's commitment to the gospel message. His teachings continue to inspire and challenge believers today, and his example serves as a powerful reminder of the transformative power of the gospel.

Chapter 6: Conclusion

The life and ministry of Paul the Apostle is one of the most inspiring and impactful stories in the history of Christianity. From his early days as a Pharisee to his conversion on the road to Damascus and his subsequent work as a missionary and teacher, Paul's journey is a testament to the power of faith, perseverance, and the transformative power of God's grace.

Throughout this book, we have explored Paul's life in depth, from his early upbringing and education to his later years as an apostle and martyr. We have examined his teachings on topics such as justification by faith, the role of grace in salvation, and the Holy Spirit's role in Christian living. We have also explored his impact on the early Christian church, from his missionary journeys to the establishment of new communities of believers.

As we bring this book to a close, it is clear that Paul's life and teachings continue to hold relevance and significance for believers today. His emphasis on faith, grace, and the transformative power of the Holy Spirit speaks to the challenges and opportunities of our own time, and his example of boldness, perseverance, and faithfulness continues to inspire and challenge us.

Above all, Paul's life and ministry remind us of the power of God's love and the transformative impact it can have on our lives and our world. Whether we are struggling with doubt, facing persecution or hardship, or simply seeking to deepen our understanding of the gospel message, Paul's teachings and example offer a powerful reminder of the enduring power of God's grace and love.

As we reflect on Paul's life and ministry, may we be inspired to continue living out the gospel message in our own lives, and may we be empowered by the same faith, hope, and love that guided Paul throughout his journey as a servant of Christ.

Lessons from Paul's Life and Ministry

Throughout the course of this book, we have examined the life and ministry of Paul the Apostle, and have seen how his example continues to hold relevance and significance for believers today. Here are some of the key lessons we can learn from his life and ministry:

1. **The power of God's grace**: Paul's conversion on the road to Damascus serves as a reminder of the power of God's grace. Despite his past as a persecutor of Christians, God saw fit to use Paul as an instrument of His message of love and salvation.

2. **The importance of faith**: Paul's teachings on justification by faith serve as a reminder that our salvation is not earned by our own efforts, but is a gift of God's grace through Jesus Christ.

3. **The role of the Holy Spirit:** Paul's emphasis on the Holy Spirit's role in Christian living serves as a reminder of the importance of allowing the Spirit to guide and empower us in our daily lives.

4. **The value of perseverance:** Paul's life was marked by numerous trials and challenges, but he never wavered in his

commitment to Christ and his mission. His example reminds us of the importance of perseverance in the face of adversity.

5. **The need for community:** Throughout his missionary journeys, Paul established numerous communities of believers who supported and encouraged one another in their faith. His example serves as a reminder of the importance of community in our own journey of faith.

6. **The call to boldly proclaim the gospel:** Despite facing persecution and opposition, Paul never shied away from boldly proclaiming the gospel message. His example challenges us to do the same, sharing the message of God's love and salvation with boldness and conviction.

Overall, Paul's life and ministry offer a wealth of lessons and insights for believers today. May we be inspired and empowered by his example, as we seek to live out the gospel message in our own lives and communities.

Continuing Impact of Paul's Teachings

Paul's teachings continue to have a profound impact on Christianity today, shaping our understanding of theology, salvation, and Christian living. Here are some examples of how Paul's teachings continue to influence believers today:

1. **The doctrine of justification by faith:** Paul's emphasis on the importance of faith in receiving salvation has been a cornerstone of Protestant theology, and has influenced the development of doctrines such as sola fide (faith alone).

2. **The role of grace:** Paul's emphasis on the role of God's grace in our salvation serves as a reminder that our salvation is not based on our own merits or good works, but is a gift of God's grace.

3. **The Holy Spirit in Christian living:** Paul's teachings on the role of the Holy Spirit in empowering and guiding believers continue to shape our understanding of the work of the Spirit in our lives.

4. **The nature of Christian community:** Paul's establishment of communities of believers, and his teachings on the importance of mutual support and encouragement, continue to shape our understanding of the role of Christian community in our lives.

5. **The importance of evangelism:** Paul's example of boldly proclaiming the gospel message, even in the face of opposition and persecution, continues to inspire and challenge believers to share the message of God's love and salvation with others.

Overall, Paul's teachings have had a lasting impact on Christianity, and continue to shape our understanding of God's redemptive work in the world. His example of faith, perseverance, and commitment to the gospel message continue to inspire and challenge believers today.

Appendix: Chronology of Paul's Life and Ministry

The chronology of Paul's life and ministry is a subject of ongoing debate among scholars, due in part to the fragmentary nature of the historical record. However, based on the available evidence from Paul's letters, the Book of Acts, and other sources, it is possible to construct a rough timeline of his life and ministry.

Here is an outline of the major events in Paul's life and ministry, arranged roughly chronologically:

c. 5-10 CE: Paul is born in Tarsus, in modern-day Turkey, to Jewish parents.

c. 30-33 CE: Jesus is crucified and resurrected.

c. 33-36 CE: The early Christian movement begins to spread in Jerusalem and other parts of the Roman Empire.

c. 35-37 CE: Saul (later known as Paul) becomes a zealous persecutor of the early Christian movement, and is present at the stoning of Stephen, the first Christian martyr.

c. 37-38 CE: According to Acts, Paul experiences a dramatic conversion on the road to Damascus, and begins to preach the gospel of Jesus Christ.

c. 38-46 CE: Paul spends several years in Arabia, and then returns to Damascus, where he begins to preach and teach in the synagogues. He also travels to Jerusalem to meet with the apostles, and is eventually sent to minister in his home region of Tarsus.

c. 46-49 CE: Paul is called by Barnabas to minister in the city of Antioch, where he begins his first missionary journey, travelling through Cyprus and Asia Minor (modern-day Turkey). He establishes several new Christian communities and begins to develop his distinctive theology.

c. 49-52 CE: Paul attends the Council of Jerusalem, where he argues for the inclusion of Gentiles in the Christian community without requiring them to follow Jewish customs. He then embarks on his second missionary journey, travelling through Greece and Macedonia.

c. 52-56 CE: Paul continues his missionary work, travelling through Asia Minor and Greece, and writing several of his epistles (including Romans and 1-2 Corinthians). He also spends some time in Ephesus, where he confronts opposition from local merchants and teaches in the school of Tyrannus.

c. 57-59 CE: Paul returns to Jerusalem, where he is arrested and brought before the Sanhedrin. He is eventually transferred to Caesarea, where he is imprisoned for two years before appealing to Caesar and being sent to Rome.

c. 60-64 CE: Paul spends several years under house arrest in Rome, where he continues to write and teach, and establishes relationships with other Christians in the city. He is eventually released, but is believed to have been re-arrested and martyred under the emperor Nero, sometime around 64 CE.

While this chronology is by no means definitive, it provides a rough outline of the major events in Paul's life and ministry, and helps us to understand the historical context in which he lived and worked.